I WONDER
AT THE PARK

BY REESE JAXON

Dedication

Inspired by my children and their friends asking lots of wonderous questions about the big world. For Mum and Jackson.

Acknowledgement

To my friends and family, a huge thank you for all your

encouragement and positive comments.

About the Author

Reese Jaxon is an incredible educator turned author! Over the past 20 years, she has taught many children to read, write and communicate effectively. Her approach, 'Read to Me - Talk to Me,' ignites a passion for reading and imagination, sparking curiosity and creativity in young minds.

Reese's debut book was inspired by a photo of her son deep in thought, it captures the essence of 'wonder'. When asked, "What are you thinking?" her son's simple response, "Just wondering," became the foundation for the book.

Look around and take in the view,
Have you seen it before or is it something new?

Look around and you will see,
Lots of things you might want to be!!

Look through the day and out at night,
Look to your left and to your right.

Look up, look down, look all around,
What wonderful things have you found?

Look up to the sky and into space,
Look at the wonder all over your face!

What are you thinking?

What do you see?

I wonder, I wonder, I wonder...

I wonder what it's like to be a... TREE?

BLOSSOMING and BLOOMING
swaying in the breeze,
Standing tall all day with ease.
My roots stuck firmly in the ground,
I'm a home full of wildlife waiting to be found.

Climbing my trunk? Don't get stuck!
Under my branches you must... DUCK!!

I wonder what it's like to be a... DUCK?

DUCKING and DIVING
on the pond all day,
Then flying high in the sky and far away.
Children will come and feed me seeds,
Sometimes I'll be hiding in the reeds.

I'm perched on a nearby log.
Look over there - can you see the... DOG?

I wonder what it's like to be a... DOG?

BARKING and BOUNDING
while fetching a twig,
Some dogs are tiny and some quite big!
I'll chase the birds and squirrels around,
Running fast my paws lift off the ground.

What an awesome sight!
Can you see children flying a... KITE?

I wonder what it's like to be a... KITE?

SWIRLING and TWIRLING
caught in the breeze,
Floating high above the park and trees.

I'm free like a bird soaring in the air,
The people below look up and stare.

Hold on tight, up up UP I fly!!
Higher and higher into the... SKY!!

I wonder what it's like to be in the... SKY?

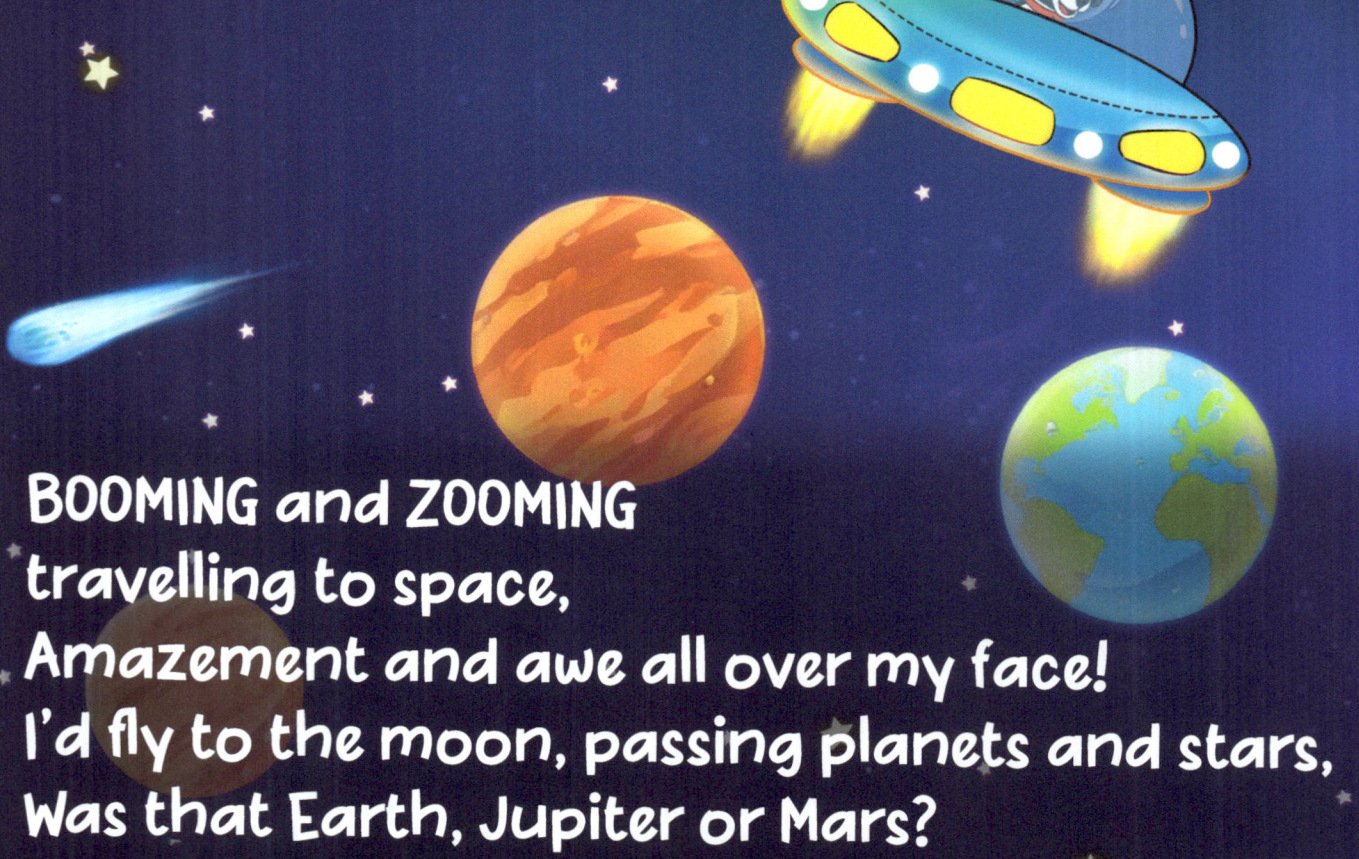

BOOMING and ZOOMING
travelling to space,
Amazement and awe all over my face!
I'd fly to the moon, passing planets and stars,
Was that Earth, Jupiter or Mars?

My WONDER has been such a BLAST,
I'm discovering a world big and so... VAST!!

My wonder has ended, my journey begun,

LAUGHING while LEARNING
and having lots of fun!

What am I thinking?

What will I be?

I wonder, I wonder, I wonder...

When I am BIG...

I will be...

Read to me... Talk to me...

Is a concept I love, it is easy to do and you don't need any training! All you need is little imagination to begin a fun conversation.

How to get the best out of this book:

Look at the illustrations and talk about what is happening on each page.
Try to predict what might happen to each character.

Example:

'Look an aeroplane!' (page 3)
'Yes, it is an aeroplane.'

Talk about it:

'Yes, that is an aeroplane. It's landing, can you see the wheels?'
Where have the passengers been?
Have you been on holiday? How did you get there? What did you pack?
What was your favourite memory?
What else flies in the sky?

Flip it:

Reverse the questions for an aeroplane taking off or flying:
Where are the passengers going?
What do you think they will see? What will they pack?
Where would you go? Have you been before?

Fit it:

'I would go to space!'
Can you go to space in an aeroplane? No, but it would be fun!
What would you need to take? What do astronauts wear?
Wonder about floating and no gravity! What would you see?

Fun activities...

Ask questions: Why is the little girl on the swing crying? What happened to the ball?
Move your body: Like a tree, a duck, a dog, a kite or pretend you are in space.
Play a game: 'I spy' or 'I see something rhyming with…' or 'I see something… RED'
Count: How many squirrels, ducks, bubbles or puddles can you find?

Most of all, have fun... wondering!!

www.ingramcontent.com/pod-product-compliance
Lightning Source LLC
Chambersburg PA
CBHW041445120626
46547CB00002B/352